THE HEART HAS A HOMELY FACE

JAMES VICTOR ANDERSON

BOOKSIDE Press

Copyright © 2023 by James Victor Anderson
ISBN: 978-1-77883-191-1 (Paperback)

All rights reserved. No part of this publication may be reproduced, distributed, or transmitted in any form or by any means, including photocopying, recording, or other electronic or mechanical methods, without the prior written permission of the publisher, except in the case brief quotations embodied in critical reviews and other noncommercial uses permitted by copyright law.

The views expressed in this book are solely those of the author and do not necessarily reflect the views of the publisher, and the publisher hereby disclaims any responsibility for them. Some names and identifying details in this book have been changed to protect the privacy of individuals.

BookSide Press
877-741-8091
www.booksidepress.com
orders@booksidepress.com

Contents

Introduction v
Wind Upon South Cove Road 1
September 2
The Seed Planter 3
Echo 4
Fleeting Meditation 5
Clutter 6
Migratory 7
Angst 8
Returning Eve 9
Clouds On The Callahans 10
Chalice 12
The Return Of War 9/11/01 13
October's Incoherence 14
Blush Wine With Turkeys 15
The Heart Has A Homely Face 17
Congregation 19
Dass Über Mich I 21
The Old North Sherman Laundry Late 40's 22
Johnny Schade 24
Strolling Through The W.C. Fields 26
Travelling Tao 27
Quiet Through A Forest Moving 28
Night Tea 29
Tao In A Teacup 30
Complaint On A Broken Meditation 31
Waiting In A Bistro Line 32
Dab Über Mich II 33
Elderage 34
To A Friend Who Quit Painting 35
Rather 37
Quiet Dancers 38
Jane Clarke's House 40
A Homely Pint 42
Bad Dates 43
Sparrow's Return 44
Village Idiot 45

Zaptoon	46
Tao Cannot Be Told	48
Shanghai Bowl Of Rice	50
Dark Stuff	51
Quiet Servant Earth	52
Moon Swallows	53
Flowering Patterned China	55
Tom	58
Tai Chi Lesson	60
Discerning The Difference	62
Sailor Mike	63
Odysseus Again	65
Madness	67
Hermit	68
In Spite Of Everything	69
Time's Apology To The Wind	71
Designated Lunatics	74
Didn't Ask You	75
The Blue Heron, Odd Ducks And Old Bloomers	76
Two Guys Bagging The Rest Of Winter	78
Zen Light	79
From The Wharf	80
Initiation To The Order	82
Mercy	83
Penguin's Wine	85
Two Poems In Memoriam To Roy Dixon Known But Through Any Man's Brother	87
II	89
Connection	90
Reclamation Of Innocence	91
About The Author	

Introduction

Perhaps it takes a single purposeness of mind to see the universe as one motion. This would be a rare thing called simplicity. It would also take years of practice to understand that Tai Chi is one motion. This is called Tao. These are aspects that the masses of humanity will never need to know. This is called homely forbearance. We need only to learn to love those faces before we meet behind the mud fence of midnight where all masks come off for the new era.

Will you look at me as one of yourselves, and say that we saw these same things together during life's long motion? Did you follow a Master who was validated from the ages of sages and prophets and teachers sent by a madman full of heaven's passion? Or did you pass us all by the roadside in a cloud of dust in the pursuit of gaining on yourself, and you haven't the slightest idea of what I'm talking about?

In the words of Omar Khayyam:
"There was a Door to which I found no Key
There was a veil past which I could not see:
Some little Talk awhile of Me and Thee
There seemed – and then no more of Me and Thee."

In this volume of poetry, I celebrate the ordinary, the

homely, mundane and awkward things that have made up the bulk of our lives, even in those extraordinary moments of achievement that to this day manifest themselves in the form of raindrops on bare wood. That is your standing ovation. But it rises to the universe in ways that we cannot know:

You alone know what it means to be a hero when no one else is watching. You alone are the critique and the correction. You may have chosen a model to work from, but what you are no longer are the pieces that fell from your emerging form. And so it went with each succeeding model, and all that which has fallen away was only that of our own creative imagination.

With any luck or grace at all you have emerged as a block of wood that was not chosen for either the sculptor's blade or the fuel gatherer's saw. Too knotted, burled and shapeless, you have been left alone to be what you are. An unshapely, cumbersome piece of work that sits just outside the mainstream of importance, and you also have the very best seat in the gallery.

Were we, then, devoid of free will, or is there a multidimensional universe that accommodates free will, and also the consequences of one's decisive actions?

In effect we have programmed our own future according to a flexible model. To be perfect like our Father in Heaven is the highest model. To comprehend our Father in Heaven is impossible, but to know yourself and find your inner balance and voice is to move toward perfection, for after all, you are not this frail body. The Masters have taught that the Kingdom of Heaven is within you. Find your point of balance, and you will have completed one motion.

Wind Upon South Cove Road

Wind waves the black wing of a dead crow
from a road tar world
like an obelisk to the dead
of long forgotten wars;
options made by ill-begotten whores
from abstract cognizance of consciousness
having not a thing to do with a choice
that listened to the vacancy of voice.
Storms tell everyone it's time to hide.
The wing that once upon the wind would ride
now rises from an earth-bound road,
beckoning to life to drop its load.
These storms return again against the coast,
reviving memory of restless ghosts
that pass through helpless by night,
and exorcised by morning's sacred light.
For now, the rain is saying wind has failed
to resurrect the crow that lies impaled
upon the mythic stele of ancient times
directed to this circle road that rhymes
with that which never has begun,
and never ends the thread spun.

September

September heat wave
Rising to a pique
Crests beneath two hawks
Circling the moon.

The Seed Planter

Old Bud Harbor knew how to grow things.
Even on his deathbed he told me,
"I didn't know how many were coming, so
I tacked an invitation to the corner tree,
and anybody turning right had to see it.
The knocking didn't stop for ninety days.
At night I threw a net to catch fish and apples
falling from the orchard by the creek.
Afterwards, the kids played 'apple core',
the folks took extra fish for home,
and those from out of town were welcome, too.
By Thanksgiving all of it was gone. I didn't ask
How many were there coming,
and that's just how many were invited.
I just kinda laugh about my share.
That's why I'm glad somebody stops and listens
'cause I have to go soon." He gave a look
And told me, "Don't forget my secret."

Goodbyes were something that he never grew

Echo

Remember
how children hid
in tall grass of vacant lots
safe inside the screen
from everything,

ladybugs grasshoppers
spiders and ants
fed a harmless garter snake,

and it all hung together
like a changing mobile
making sense out of stars
emerging from adults
becoming darkness,

and if the mother's voice
is time that carries
far beyond that place,

it's time to head
for home again.

Fleeting Meditation

Bare feet splash
over smooth stones
lying shallow
in a busy stream;
and I doubt that even
in a fallow dream that anything
could run as quiet
as this silent meditation
passing like the feet of children
running into distant darkness.

Clutter

Peering through an alley
of my childhood,
I could see some clutter
at the other end
that looked like wooden
lawn furniture
or a row of mailboxes,
(I couldn't tell)
and a crow laughed loud enough
that it made no difference.

Migratory

A wave of yellow finches
lights upon heavy heads of grass.
One more ceremonial feeding
before autumn passes over peaks
of well extended granaries,
and messages by word
of migratory beaks
whistling far as spreading
through the Urals reach
before this golden horde descends
upon the fields of Genghis Khan,
nourished by the seed that fills
this future moving on.

Angst

Half-moon floating
through sundown maples
lights an image
on a blue morning pond
as crisp, late October air
hangs beneath a balustrade,
nipping green tomatoes
clinging desperately
toward completion.

Returning Eve

Lovely young mother
framed in chestnut hair,
explaining to her child the change
of seasons for familiar trees,
and reasons for exiled birds
and empty nests,
why cats must grow their winter vests
and maples flitter theirs away,
beheld her child about to say
that fall goes early out of style,
exchanging from the forehead
to the softer dropping of an apple
on a nightdream winter smile,
asleep that Good and Evil make a liar
out of one another
like the arbitrary witches that we cast
upon a fire.

Clouds On The Callahans

What's the sound
of heavy mist pouring
over forest hills?

Does it sound like breakers
detonating over cliffs embracing
to Shore Acres?

Or, does it sound like artillery,
loud and shrill,
burying again the dead
who won't lie still?

Maybe it just sounds like feelings die
when frog and cricket concerts
suddenly run dry.

Does it purr like the cat
that loves its belly rubbed,
or is it like a tumor spreading
to the brain its vicious rumor?

And maybe it's the salve
Prometheus on the rocky face
shall never have.

So, what's the sight of sifting clouds
to do with mortal men?
Nothing, in the sense of other than
we see things of ourselves upon the land.

For what do clouds sifting over hills care
About your market gain
pouring down a steep terrain
in long and wispy arms of mist
fading like an amethyst?

There's no stock in this
but the mirror of the soul, the eye,
investing for itself those things
that never die.

What do mists sifting over hills
have to do with whether
you are good or ill?

Not a thing,
unless you've never known
the subtle sounds they sing.

Chalice

Listening to ourselves,
we may hear that we are not
at all religious now,
but more like wounded spirits
rankling in a house of prayer,
and though we sing
is not the point
compared to how we once
were spent to midlife's change,
and so the soul demands to know
from whence our feelings come,
and just to find
what love is not
completely fills this empty cup.

The Return Of War
9/11/01

A horsetail sugar sky
sprays over royal blue countertops,
swept like cream rolling
through four-dimensional coffee.
Red Tail Fokkers
and Sopwith Buzzards dogfight
over a spreading cold front.

Everywhere rats advance,
and Christmas decorations rise.

We are doomed to repeat ourselves.

I am too old to fight now.
I must find peace within myself.

I return to my meditations,
Stretches and Tai Chi.

October's Incoherence

October is the culmination
of the spring and summer's
touching winter,
and just before the edge of fall
its golden incoherence
is a metaphor
of silky cats that slip around
an unlatched door,
or worse, a dear departed uncle
in another family's hearse,
but slanting snow
down hillside alders,
I'm afraid, will cover up
my summer dream of singing jade,
but if it please the seasons to provide
one month expressive of the rest,
then October's incoherence
wears the Jack O'Lantern's jest.

Blush Wine With Turkeys

Drinking blush wine with turkeys
under a new moon
focuses light
through children's eyes.

And so my neighbor's child
made her wish upon
this heavenly wedge,
and putting down my goblet
let her know this thing
is merely the fingernail of God,
for once a month He clips one nail
and sends it flying across the sky.

Foraging turkeys raise their dinosaur domes
to gawk at my vulnerable lapse of mind
while my neighbor mumbles epithets
concerning child hating bulshitters
telling his kid a thing like that

but hey, I'd like the kid to know
that God is never in a hurry but
always on time,
and offset all the "better" knowledge
she'll have to see through later on.

I shout through the underbrush of things
that grow against the grain,
or why would I be drinking blush wine
with turkeys?

The Heart Has A Homely Face

I really don't know
what they were thinking
two short high school girls
not in a beauty race at all,
running down Harvard Boulevard,
hair merging with wind
like Vasco deGama making his point,
laughing into noise
that might as well have been a rickshaw
running Groucho Marx to Roseburg,
and I don't know what they were thinking
out there running in the wind
like it really didn't matter
if an orphan had a black eye
or a frayed and faded scarf
about a blemished cheek was furled,

for I remember soldiers on a weekend
roaming Monterey's peninsula
and who simply had to get away
from all the voices telling how
we'd have to die to make the world go 'round,
and we looked pretty homely
next to sky upon Pacific hills of oak and moss,
not a privileged set

embracing sweetness
in the pearls of blonded smiles,
or lightning Grecian paths through college miles.
No, we were drab eternal to the fields,
And I don't know what we were thinking
Running off from home like that.

And so, two short high school girls
traverse the crosswalk now against the light,
and I stop to let them stretch for home.

For just this moment
there are only homely faces on their way
to praise the scarred Acropolis,
and kiss the battered face of chance
the silent Sphinx has borne.

Congregation

At the beginning
of the Father's sermon
rain began to fall

As his sermon reached
the crux of its thesis
rain gutters began to leak

At his conclusion
water spilled as smoothly
as over a dam

After service
the congregation moved
and seconded
bids for new rain troughs

This was not seen
as a problem

I mean
why wouldn't there have been water?

It was spontaneous
And we rose to guide it
to the better outcome

We follow the Christ.
We are Tao.

Dass Über Mich I

I cannot tell you
what the soul is made of.

It's everything you've seen rescinded
in a childhood made floating on the wind
outside a classroom window over dust
and leaves that mushrooms in a field believe
in mud puddle broths,
and cobwebbed morning dew that clings
to the faintest background noise that sings
its undecipherable chant that someone
deep inside hears as you pass, and next,

you're all alone in class.

The Old North Sherman Laundry Late 40's

Raggedy urchins draped in drab
depression hand-me-ups that stab
and stain the staircase in pursuit
of falling in the laundry chute.
Manned by mothers cast aside
by a changing world in a rising tide,
reflecting in my pathos pool
forever walking home from school,
those staring, rude, neglected cries
in childish dark and dirty eyes
where there's no help in scalding steam
to answer falling children's screams.
The irony falls on little girls
with yellowed hair too short for curls,
and one with a crumbling storybook
reads aloud to vacant looks
huddled on an upper step,
a sarcophagus likened Imhotep
to poverty well preserved by stealth
in those tiny womb's inherent wealth,
and I watched them grow
from this tiny class
to a 21st Century social mass

with empty stares, the plaintive cries,
the glassy love forgotten eyes,
the stumbling knowledge in their looks,
the artificial wealth of books,
the clever make-up hiding dirt
smeared upon the hidden hurt,
and everybody hides the shame
by holding someone else to blame,
and every victim filing suit
is recompense from the laundry chute.

Johnny Schade

I caught up to Johnny Schade going home
from school one autumn afternoon,
and I knew him by his absence for so long
that I yelled, "Johnny, where've you been?"
but down his head was hung as he replied,
"No, ya don't wanna talk to me. Ya better off
to think I must've died."

But errant schoolboys always give rebuttal.
"Hardly no one ever knew you, Johnny, but you and me
had lots of fun together running loose in games of tag
with rules we made our own, around one way and then
another, fast as we could turn and yell 'ya can't catch me'
inside the game we had a secret name for".

And in a moment Johnny almost quite forgot he smiled,
he met the flicker of his rising eyes just long enough
to laugh and say we did have fun, he told me that
we can't be friends because his life is different now,
and getting worse. "Why don't you know
I've been in jail, and going to reform school next?"

I plead I didn't know or ever heard, and can't believe
that he could ever be that bad, like things will always
turn around, I wanted to convince myself,
but Johnny knew, and like an older brother dying young

he smirked and said, "You don't know nothin'. I gotta go."
Stepping out with longer strides he left me there
between the street and what he never had for home,
his slapping feet repeating like the lashes on a helpless back,
the backhand slap across a ruddy cheek, boy I knew
who loved to run and laugh with no tomorrows turning
rancid like his sorry back receding
down the long perspective of a gutter.

And that's the last I saw of Johnny Schade until the day
he came to hang around our school, and cops just came
to haul him off again; that long, rebellious hair accenting
laughter gone insane and crying, "All a'you are fuckin' bastards",
and by his shackled arms they took him in a final tag, you're it.

Among the spat good riddances I wanted just to cry
you never knew him, and now you'll never know,
but I knew it wouldn't wash against the pride of glad
contempt, and later when I read that he'd been shot
while trying to run away, I promised that I always would
remember Johnny standing lonely in a vacant lot,
back pockets full of hands in waiting for my signal
to begin the game.

Strolling Through The W.C. Fields

Ahhh, yeeeeees. Respectability.
The last refuge of scoundrels,
bushwackers, and the mainstay
of good ol' boy cronyism.
And mostly fools think
it's better than rum.

Travelling Tao

I never need to see
where I go.
I follow what hills
And mountains know,
And never betray their wills.

So many religionists like to tell
how blindly I'm lost
and going to hell,
yet rarely they see
that heaven or hell
at some point will unravel
unless they come to understand
that each is a way of travel.

I'd rather take
the curve or crest,
and pass on judgment which is best,

for I never need to see
where I go,
and I'll never reach the end,
you know.

Quiet Through A Forest Moving

Under sprays
of snow illumined light
spicy leaves decay upon winter grass,
and under mossy boughs and trunks
oozing amber oils of scented wood
drift on crosswinds
over lichen crusted boulders,
wafting pungency just
above a hidden stream
running through a prophecy of mist
that blesses on a day that goes
without the falcon's piercing cry, still
like snowdrifts at the timber kneeling
softly on a cushion sewn of pine.

Spirits pass
like puffs of breath,
and meditate the quiet
through a forest moving

Night Tea

The glare of harshest winter light
softens in a stormy night
upon a swirling eddy spun
within a dark bone china cup.
Ragged edges outline change
That upward turn to drink us up,
and leaving at a table bare
of anything that makes aware
that night remembers who we were
before the tea begins to stir
and settle in a granule spray
depositing another day.

Tao In A Teacup

A circle
whose center
is everywhere and
circumference nowhere
better illustrates
that there is no Very God
where there is only Very God.

Complaint On A Broken Meditation

Down a sea cliff path they gawk,
smacking of feet
and pedestrian talk:

"The ocean's rough today.
See how high the breakers,
how tall the wind-shaped trees,
and the sea sounds the echo
of a dying god."

Only no one really says it that way
beyond a mockery, and made today a shitstick
of the English tongue and Tao.

Why must it be said
why point your finger at the moon?
You deny its voice,
and so, before something out there
calls your name to live among
redundant things all run together,

close your oafish mouth
and cockeyed stare.
Everything's one motion,
and you missed it there.

Waiting In A Bistro Line

Mankind will next evolve
to a public place of silence
where patrons fill a room
to dine while tyrants stand
ten thousand years behind
the scratchy leaf that just blew in
across the doorsill on the sort
of April breeze that everybody
sees at once,
and knowing it says everything
without the tongue's elusive hunts.
So quiet will we breathe
that streams a mile away
shall echo in our veins
that weave the way we find
a common thread throughout mankind.
Impatient rancor
will be limited to arctic ice,
and war confined to whom shall yield
a melon slice.
but none shall every say a word,
and so let all men stare
at what shall someday come
of the public standing there.

Dab Über Mich II

So many friends I love
have died this winter,
and powdered snow blowing
through dry gardens
whispers something secret
to deep perennial roots.

Elderage

Senescence
lurks like
a cat shadow
crouched against
the dark side of Tuesday
waiting for the memory
of a bird to pass its way,
and hungry since the master died
it must forage for itself
upon the ghosts of things
already passed.

To A Friend Who Quit Painting

Those few flowers
pushing up between
the grasses in your field

the same number
of original ideas you ever had
in your life

better mow them now
before you have remembered
what you came to struggle for

and how easy it has been to go
along the shallow edges
where it's clear and closer
in the sight of friends

and now you've never been alone

but if you want to paint
as poets write
then either sink into the green
and murky water where no one
wants to follow Beowulf,
or cringe when blood comes roiling
to the top

you know the very hero whom you are
when no one else is watching
or will ever know

but those few flowers
pushing up between
the grasses in your field
better mow them now

Rather

Cloning another human
is about as B Western
as a shootout where
nobody really wins
because no one
got the girl.

Quiet Dancers

Robert went to school
when everything
was hung upon
the social scale
of Damocles,
but searching out
the why of things
had branded him Diogenes.

And then he asked
one girl to dance
whose affliction was
she had no voice,
and had to whisper her consent
that he could barely hear,
and closely to her bent.

Together they composed
a quiet dance I still recall
since forty years spontaneous to the temperament
of other's staring grip,
the small, the mean and petty
who are always there to make us slip.

But on a floor of liquid light
Her motions laughed

like asters in the wind
against his sail,
and to make her any more than that
would merely fail
their quiet dance.

Forever in that evening
he is current of her sea,
and she whispered
in his dying ears
everything the wind could be.

Jane Clarke's House

Very much she was the house she lived in,
a dignified simplicity of lines that ran straight
and down to earth, compartmentalized inside
to purposes yet unknown, devout
to her perennial wildflowers that still survive
as buffers from the world and sentinels
to her quiet morning call to chapel.

The tidy world in which she dwelled had worn
transparent to a wryness of her face,
and she always looked as if she knew a thing
you'd never find, so it's disconcerting
as the puzzled missing pieces of her well worn
Karmen Ghia that no longer makes its power mower
fits and starts through town, and I wonder who
inherited her leather trademark hair barrette
that always held her salt and pepper style that way.

Kindness in her eyes was the only other interest
to contest her will; one has to earn a thing like that,
as none can ever give the house you lived in to another
who never understood the love that lived inside,
and that's what makes her house appear to sad
without her in it now, as something's dull about the paint
and lines that blur with listless trees that hang around

the place like school is out but no one's home.
Jane's house is still a place to marvel,
but I wish that everyone could understand
that grandness of the dwelling one inhabits
is a thing that death does not disband.

A Homely Pint

The last I saw of winter
rolling over windowsills
was poring over dinner
and a pint of ale on shadows
filtered through from fall,
and as I overlooked the freight yard
framed in branches meant to bud their way
through March and into May,
I stopped my breath and motion
for all the earth and life that feels
upon my tongue with deep devotion
as a man of mud gone fishing
in a world of sin is sat,
for what more judgment can be brought
against a simple man than that?

Bad Dates

but when I gave the punch line
'bout the bullfrog sitting
on the guy's head

it went right over hers
and left the frog still sitting there

well, it was an awkward moment
stirring coffee till it's cold
and spilling change to show
I'm clumsy too

and leaning over sideways picking
up the fallen coins I prayed
I wouldn't fart

And find that sitting up again
I'm all alone

hello

Sparrow's Return

I felt a movement
just beneath my garden shrubs
as if the universe
had been displaced
by seven centimeters.

Some tiny thing
went running underneath
my rhododendrons
like a spirit hiding
just behind a smiling cat.

Kneeling down then,
I could see that it was
only poet Takahashi dancing
on his sparrow legs,

for Spring is but a month away,
and I've clutched his leaves
in my warm fingers
since December.

Village Idiot

How relieved I was
to find others
more knowledgeable than me,
and how ignorant I really am.

My friend Lao-Tzu told me
how all knowledge has existed
quite before I ever was,

but now how lonely
that I'm even dispossessed
of knowing that.

How could I have known
without any light, that water
reflects the darkness of night?

Zaptoon

If I would make
my own animated 'toon
I'd have Ebenezer Scrooge
cornering the wurst market,
sending sausage stocks soaring
through global exchanges worldwide,
and starvation would be no more,
love and peace would break out
like incurable teenage acne,
and there would be dancing and singing
and kissing and frisbee contests
with old Elvis records,
and people with children would learn
thoughtful manners while rock groups
formed quiet meditation bands,
and organized religions and armies
went bankrupt just like dentists
who taught the whole world to brush
and floss and even Gottihmselbst
would be at such loss.
No flood, no fire, no armageddon
to conspire against our future hopes.
My 'toon would end with everybody
picking up our world and running with it,

just like ants at a picnic.
That's all, folks.

Tao Cannot Be Told

Jim O'Neill,
your book of poetry weighs heavier
upon my shelf of sages.
I welcomed times we worked together
over paper strewn tables holding up
our best intentions meant for those thereafter.
I remember you leaning over light reflections
floating on our work table, almost
like you saw the river in a light
that hurt your eyes
I cherished times that we drank together,
dangling by laughter in the wind,
dueling Death Ihmselbst with
little plastic swizzle sticks,
and it all came out grammatical.
Men who teach English always come out Zen.
Your book of poems is easiest to find.
It's the only one without a title on its spine.
It forms one black slot between the sages
pointing toward the untold pages.
How Zen of you, O'Neill,
to remember us like this.
I see you grinning,
and when I take you down to read

I'll see you laughing back at me
because I find you nameless
among the other things.

Shanghai Bowl Of Rice

Rising warmth
over cold water
waiting just above the navel,
steam rises now like breath
that nurtures every grain
on mornings fraught with ice,
that rice sustains
almost the world's
dependency on nimble hands
and empty bowls go begging
just to fill with heat that rises
from the steaming back
of labor's mortal realm.

But once upon a time
had farmers sown their rice
more preciously than gold
or virgins passing safely
on their way,
that now a bowl of rice
can buy the solar cycle
one more day.

Dark Stuff

Darkness is a substance
I can swing my arms through
like a Sou'wester hurricane night
that carries me in its wine swirled cup,
and sometimes, just before
the dawn comes up,
I go outside and gather all the dark I can
to stuff the spirit mattress where I rest
upon that thin division of a padding
keeping me abreast of things.
And when the darkness
after many restless nights
becomes the flattened shadow of myself,
I go outside before the dawn succeeds,
and gather one more armload
for the rest I need.

Quiet Servant Earth

Rock faced hill
under a cloudy hood
likens to a hermit monk emerging
from the deeper years of wilderness.
Branchlet hands clutching cold fish
are breakfast graced
by early morning's glassy plate,
the shivering cold of love the spice
that covers particles of hate,
and like the warming later in the day,
and hooded monk must rise and turn away,
and ply his service to a spirit world
dispensing of itself through all our lives
like shadows longing for mortality,
reaching through the afternoons as knives
that pare the time about our core
until we've begged the hermit monk
to let us pass this way for more.

Moon Swallows

Sure, and I remember
that the moon was always there
before the promises were made,
and I remember swallows
skimming closer
to a moon reflected lake
than love was ever called,
and I can still recall
when men looked deep into the lake
themselves, unafraid
of time and close affection
with the past, and every challenge
coming fast was game
at turning slowly
as an eye that wakes
from tender sleep
where moons and swallows guide
the mortal kind transcending
to their higher selves
from careless, tired routines that drive
the patient to their ends,
like here,
upon our simple, petty paths
we leave behind that no one

wants to follow
is everything we still must hope
attracts the migrant moon swallow
to the hidden, crevassed edge of fear,
and nurture more to come
for nesting here.

Flowering Patterned China

Deep, massive current
moving calmly,
placid as Pacific isles,
or peasant garden fields
on an overwhelming ocean
daubed of straw
and bentwood huts
long shadowed on the city's outskirts,
towering like the Buddha's jutting fingers
to the very clouds, holding commerce
to the worldly crowds.

Change now writes
the law of China
whose dragon supercedes
the falling walls
about an ancient world's angina.
Change is certain
As the ocean tide, and change
is only disobeyed
by those who've died.

China, rising
on its massive humanity,
its social classes spreading

like a forest filtered light
upon the deep
of unspoiled faces
full with hope that wake
like innocence aroused
from sleep.

A heavy drone of power
hums beneath its urban streets
like drums resounding
from the ancient courts of Khans,
but driven from the fingertips
of lighter souls in glowing heights
that illustrate the night
like science fiction written
without pretense
of some growing doom within.

But China grows from that
already rooted in the Tao
left behind from millions
of ancestral minds
contributing to now.

Distinctive as the herbs and rice
are savored, not a man
or salvaged bit of thing is wasted
in this rising world
that's kept its promises to those
who've borne the weight disposed

to liberate a people's name.

A longer March
than recent memory knows
this China in the early spring
where impressionistic points of green
come healing from the Northern wall,
from Beijing snow, to Shanghai winds,
to humid Kowloon and Hong Kong
it grows upon the faces of a people
marching into time that waited through
a maelstrom history for this moment
just to smile in retrospect
the very universe all men
of common good
reflect.

Tom

I know a man who has no bones,
and walks the way the sea intones
with undulating waves that move
in steps that physics cannot prove,
that he could pass between the rhyme
of reason in between the time
it takes to quickly glance away,
return and find him gone astray
from where he stood
and should have been
but moving out of time again
between the pulse as time exists
through universal amethysts
conveying laser beams of light
subtracting day by adding night,
but he was there in full accord
as solid as his moving toward
my hand to shake, my voice to hear
as real as any drawing near
a friend familiar to the eye
or recognition of the sky,
or hears the upper winds that moan
about my flesh, about my bone,
and I've meditated long and prayed
for dedication still delayed

to learn to move without my bones,
and walk the way the sea intones.

Tai Chi Lesson

Walking like a cat
is the hardest thing to learn,
and it's harder like
you lose a friend.

A young athlete, the older warrior
and the walking meditative scholar,
had all undone my later years.

Those pillars of strength
advancing my feet were machinations
fusing bone and joint
that cannot stand when earth turns
upon its softer feline paws.

So my ankles were the knotted burls
that merely bind the falling tree.

But how do I learn the walk of a cat
like the first step
of a thousand miles?

Ah, there, through my gate
comes old Tiger Eyes
with a fresh mouse dangling,

and for a bowl of milk he'll teach me

till the day that I outlive his lessons.
And how hard it will be then
to lose a friend.

Discerning The Difference

A Taoist and a Buddhist
walked into a teahouse
and ordered pots of tea.

The Taoist ordered green tea,
and the Buddhist ordered black,
and gravitated to the only
empty table at the back,
and placed their pots and cups
and sat.

After a moment of silence
the Taoist poured his green tea
into the Buddhist's cup,
and in a minute of consideration
the Buddhist poured his black tea
into the Taoist's cup.

Having the Taoist's attention,
The Buddhist asked, "At which point
did it occur to you that we should
share each other's tea?"

And the Taoist slowly replied,
"I don't know.
We were never invited."

Sailor Mike

Mike was terminal now,
a mystery in a wing backed chair,
another victim of malignant plots
    against eternal life

and once he owned a farm and ran it,
    could ride and rope and, shoot,
for all I know distributed the best DNA
far countrywide, for he had a kindness
    in his eyes that said
    the ladies came to him

and he had farm machines and trucks that
he'd dismantled twice two hundred times
repaired and meetings ran at his house
    when the grange hall burned
and he knew commodities exchanged
and moved his share far out ahead of most
and sold mail ordered health food seeds
    to Californians scared of growing old

and once some sixty years ago
ducked a kamikaze coming straight for him

    his sudden eyes now turn to me
and ask why this has had to happen now

and something came to me that I replied
that long before we're born here
we agree to these conditions

and his eyes rolled back in older recognition
that made him right with that
Mike peacefully expired next day
And I know he knew the way
Before the kamikaze hit

Odysseus Again

And in my comfortable old field jacket
that I could have wrapped forever in,
and wives bemoan that men should never
wear to town,

we entered the cathedral, and I,
I was handed cans of food
by the well-intended mission lady.

"No, wait, we're here for the bookstore.",
I then reply with a somewhat twitching
of the eye, and my wife returned
with some distress those cans of food
I tried to press away from view
without her catch I told you so
in haunting eyes that match.

"But it's not the coat that
makes me look like homeless.",
I bandied with her later.
"It's just the way I look, in the eyes,
the step. I could have worn a tux
and she'd have handed food to me."
"The coat's gotta go.",
she then replied, and somewhere
on the streets of Portland goes

my last remnant of the mighty Sixth Army
up in arms of listless cadence
of the derelict.

And I thought of Odysseus off again,
twenty years to find his way, disguised
the homeless beggar, slew the suitors
coveting his home and wife, and how
Penelope then pushed the test one more.

Madness

Subatomic rumbling
horse hooves
and armored treads
grind together
grit of dry wastelands.

Rising through the legs
it tells
sane men to turn and run.

The worst of men
cheer from the sidelines,
goading those
who hold
their ground.

The best of men
still lying
in the wastelands

amplify their elements
in the subatomic rumble.

Hermit

Before you walk
five sacred mountains
to separate the fountains
from the madness,
settle first inside like sand is sinking
slowly where the water lies.
Wait until it's fallen to the bottoms
of your legs,
then set your course into insidious days
with solid, steady stride outpacing even distances
apocalyptic horsemen ride.
Action rises with spontaneous dust,
and you shall guide its outcome as you must,
for you have followed Tao where you have been,
and live among the masses
as a hermit among men.

In Spite Of Everything

Most old friends are gone now,
and the aging mother missed the satisfaction
of having not outlived her children.
The wife recites insurance odds
that she'll survive into that fearful senescence
of woman's awful vigilance.
All threats that never came to pass
stare through a picket fence, waiting to be fed.
So what if life was never fair, but never was it more
than I could learn to balance in the working limits
of my arms, and in spite of everything
spring returns the colors of every joyful touch
that it exhorts to give another,
and the Marches through our future winters
only show that bright.
In spite of everything
the meaningful analogies of death
are buried in the potter's field of Death's choosing;
Death chooses the remains of what life comes to mean,
and so it makes me wish I'd learned more dances,
wear obnoxious ties and baggy pants
to anybody's wedding, funeral,
juggling shrunken heads a baptism,
hire a drunken Swede to sing the Barber of Seville

on Groundhog's Day for god's sake or sing
with mermaids on the rocks of my own
carelessness,
to die in the sexual caress of kelp and scuttling claws.
That is how the sirens sing for me, T.S.,
in spite of everything,
and all the English poetry and masterful delusions
float upon the water of its own urination
until kidney failure takes this body
from the foul ecclesiastic shorts
that ride us to the edge of madness.
And when your NCO from Hell comes out to say,
I want everybody out and in formation at 0600 hours
wearing all your dirty laundry over that civy clean body
you thought you owned, you're mine again, and
I'm gonna teach you to forget everything you ever thought
you knew!", then you'll know Death's like that,
and in spite of everything, reasonable
in perspective of never having lived at all,
but, hey, foxgloves say it so much better
here and now than a cheap pencil and a cup of tea
dribbling on a legal pad,
and spring is always rather than
the death we've never seen.

Time's Apology To The Wind

I do not hear you
while I'm busy rushing,
and I listen very closely.
I'd rather hear myself
about my business anyway
than feel you mutely
like a rock beneath the water
on its course.

What does time have to say
after forty years of silence?
Was there something that you said?
Would you tell me that you love me
or my money when I'm dead?

Or did it matter that I rattled
through your house like bones
still hiding in a secret place?

I can't remember,
and you mumble so
like captains lost
in nursing homes.

But I don't hear you
while I'm roaring through

the girders of your spine
and blur your vision
cold with brine.

I remember now,
your wanting to empower yourself
by telling me how much
you hold me in contempt,
the vicious pleasure
dripping from your eyes
the size of hate that spits
between the teeth.

I remember you now,
enmeshed in all the lies
that others told you
for their gain.

But what did you get?

I know I never heard from you again
when I went howling through
my arctic nights
so long ago.

And now you wish to say
you're sorry,
that you need to be forgiven
to alleviate the pain.

And does it really make
a difference if I do?

If you've hauled the corpse this far
what makes you think
I'll bury it for you?

I'm only thankful that I've power
to blow the stench away.
And, all right, I forgive you
for having said those things
I said I never heard. So,
you can go in peace,
but I'd rather that we'd gone
for beer and maybe just
a game of handball.

But I know that you can't hear me
now above the rising sigh
lifting all that bulk of guilt.

For forty years
I kept my secret hanging
on a dagger's point.
It doesn't matter now.
The wind is just a way
that time erodes the memory
of itself.

Designated Lunatics

Determined to illustrate just how the universe
is strung together with a humorous punchline,
Delano strapped himself with dynamite
and detonated his sorry ass at the center
of a well-known California winery.
Months later a woman screamed and fainted
in a San Fransisco wine bar when she asked
her bartender to pour three fingers,
and she got them.
Nobody laughed,
and you were wrong, Delano
but we pickled your middle finger anyway,
just to make your point.

Didn't Ask You

Reflecting
in the slough side of noon,
one fisherman in waders
casting like
he didn't give a rat's ass
if World War I still raged
about him like someone else's problem
can't be fixed
by going fishing, damn it.

Go away.

The Blue Heron, Odd Ducks And Old Bloomers

Elder matrons waddle
By a bistro window
quacking at the pastry looking flowers
one might think were baked inside
the window box,
and pointing feathery fingers
like the dilettantes of diets
so the more of them come running
in a quack excitement
set on being first to see it blooming
right beside my poultry plate
adjacent to that bistro window
where most patrons
eating continental freudery
just inside as older women outside
went to chasing butterflies
that try to light upon
the iris, pansy upturned faces luring
raucous womenfolk this sunny noontide
by a 19th Century bay
forgotten in the letters
filigreed upon some flaking dockside store
gone begging for a handout from the guy

who took the risk to build a bistro with a window planter
bringing every ducky lady squabbling
over who shall name the flower
on this moment swept
by feathery wings
that hover by this planter box of May.

Two Guys Bagging The Rest Of Winter

February, fleet
across a violet horizon,
cleaves months of gray,
and aqua green
stains the water
where heads of kelp
in whitecaps wave,

but now two stealthy men
along a coastal trail
carry a wooden spar
with a plastic bag
suspiciously suspended
in a way

anyway,
they amble on
talking low and secret,
careful not to catch an eye,
nondescript in dress,
but shouts rebellion
that you cannot prove,

and back upon the road
nobody saw them leave,
but most of March is gone.

Zen Light

Mud turtles stretch-necked
in the sun,
bask with no permission
on a log that floats without it, too.

From The Wharf

From the wharf
I watched a fisherman
hip deep in fish and laughing
like he loved the whole melee around him
singing subatomic silver particles stackled
by Gottihmselbst in raucous laughter like
every fisherman is somewhat "tetched" like
Peter present at the feeding of five thousand,
standing on the rock of Rome and wondering
why two-thousand twisted years of sin filled
laters that we've come to this,
and I watched the joy of a hip deep fisherman
who simply fed his own from what he pulled
together, but the statue of a saint's a lonely thing
like a grandpa that you never knew, but
he was grand and gave his watch and chain for you,
and it clanks and rattles like the vessels
of the elements upon a Sunday morning
that has meaning now that I've got
Lao-Tzu's Tao te Ching inside my suit coat
and the fact that no one knows it's there's
the secret Jesus tried to show us that
the love inside does not require a miracle
or words or fish forgotten

with a holy kingdom of decay that really was
intended for recycle in a world like this,
and wouldn't it be really some surprise
if something unexpected grew from this;
A secret everybody keeps inside, never to reveal
by solemn oath that something shining
from the inside out that everybody else can see
from every wharf where everybody deep in fish
can stand upon the rock of Rome and feed
the thousands come to hear a lesson
having had no name or words to understand,
and the laughing, joy filled fisherman
is just a man who woke this morning
full of sure anticipation
that you were on
the wharf today,
and we both depended
on each other's
being there
for the meaning
that we are.

Initiation To The Order

There was a secret trail along a sandstone bank,
carved by local kids to try the loyalty of friends.
The trail traversed the length of town,
and kept in good repair
by members of their secret order
known to one another only by a special sign.
To learn the sign one had to walk the trail
with hands in pockets while the other boys
hurled pine cones or an apple core
to test his nerve.
But, acceptance in that league was something
tantamount to serving Arthur's table.
The saddest boys were those unstable
with their footing,
rolling twenty feet to reach a swampy mess,
and subject to the laughter and the taunts
that to this day the memory haunts, I'd guess.
But one thing sure we carried with us
since those daring boyhood escapades
that never leave our judgment's sight:
We learn because we make a choice,
and not because we get it right.

Mercy

In retrospect
to the all-protective ego,

we are small,
not very bright,
and funny looking as coconuts go
in the universal scheme of things olympic.

Have mercy on our false hopes
that the hangman's after
the other guy.

Have mercy on
the self-protected coward
swinging rhythmically in
jaybird laughing wind.

Bury him under the heroes
for whom he wouldn't
lift a finger.

For all that are left now
are the homely, the funny looking
the quirky in the quarks of physics.

Protect us from those
who will rise up to say
that they are not so,

to lead us into better times.

Even the stone mountain
echoes from its quarry
we are not to be trusted.
Have mercy on us, Quan Yin,
growing funny in our little corner.

Penguin's Wine

Passing through the rain
like penguins pouring wine
go things we never say we see,
and sometimes like I feel the pain of no one there
I go to places where they used to be
and find the set was struck
so long ago
not even was a memory
of their presence found,
that time had taken issue with the past
and left it in a foundry
for the present mold to cast,
but not the dice of chance gone tumbling
over roughened felt,
or can one hour of dance bring back
those partners when the cards were dealt.
We're gone, we've fled.
The world has turned against
our field of flowers,
and spread its seeds of promise
over cold, gray stone.
I peer through windows smeared with rain
while passing down our streets alone,
and insulated from the chance

that someone there is calling me
from one familiar door and old café
where nothing came of what there used to be.
And so today I feel like pain,
but no one's there, and all the old connections
that once had tied familiar circuits
to directories that reach
the common nerves that far away are sped
on websites where the preference is
we leave the dead
who cannot say hello or clasp a hand
or shoulder with the gasp of true surprise,
or find in decades later that we never knew
each other's soul within the eyes.
We just aren't there where once we ran away
to find our far revealing paths,
and while we may have hoped all roads
would intertwine again,
it still remains that all the loneliness
that's ever been
has taken place of empathy,
and only those who've given love in grace
have tasted wine that penguins pour
from mortal pain.

Two Poems In Memoriam To Roy Dixon Known But Through Any Man's Brother

Some afternoon so quiet
you can hear the warm air rise
we'll take a boat downstream
to where the water cries
in silent pools of light
standing too polite to move
and stir an afternoon so still
that sir, I think I'll go and rest
upon the troubles of my chest
that soften in the silence
of the shadows of the moon
that move about my circle
like a broom removing cobwebs
from the hanging hemlock boughs
that brush the river where
we've drifted for awhile,
and if we've gone an inch
I'd say we've gone a mile
considering we first came in
the other way without a sound
and made it to the other side,
and no one drowned.
The air's so still I hear the tap

on holographic window panes
beside my nap, and
one afternoon so quiet
we'll take a boat downstream
and float upon the silence
of a reoccurring dream.

II

Earth eternally blowing into place
becomes a giant heap of leaves
against the sacred mountains,
and the leap of faith through space
lands softly on its balance
while old Lao-Tzu himself surfs
through stars of Jesus laughter skimming
Earth as lightly as the snow that floated
through the open door of yesterday,
and down upon the current wind
that followed all our futures to a place
we risked our very souls to live
upon a windy cradle,
cover us now, and let us sleep.

Connection

And you shall hold the dying in your arms
to hear the failing breath expire
that you are not so far behind.
Cherish that unbroken silence with your eyes.
Long shadows of an afternoon reach across
the road you travel, flickering as you pass
the river running on beside you
as it has so many times before,
and shall return again for more.
Only bridges need rebuilding now.
We ride on currents to the sea and wonder
where the boundaries used to be,
like someone dying waking in your arms,
and rising through the bones of your alarms.

Reclamation Of Innocence

Like wind beneath a butterfly
unseen against an empty sky
is life's long echo of the fall
of nothing, nothing there
at all.

About The Author

James Victor Anderson is a native of Southwestern Oregon. He was born August 24th, 1940 to the coastal towns of North Bend/Coos Bay, and grew up on the Coos Bay waterfront during the pinnacle of the lumber and fishing industries. During the late fifties he served in the U.S. Army Intelligence Corp with the XVIII Airborne, and with the Oregon National Guard's 249th Artillery during his college years at Linfield College where he earned his BA in English/Literature and a Masters in English-Education. James served as a high school and college teacher in Oregon's toughest logging region of Southern Douglas County, and was named five times to Who's Who Among American Teachers.

James now lives in the relative quietness of Roseburg, Oregon with his very loving artist wife Donna Marie, who says she doesn't understand poets but accommodates him, nevertheless. In retirement James has previously written and published two books of poetry in the Taoist perspective, titled NOT UNLIKE A MADMAN IN CHEAP SANDALS, and DANCE WITHOUT A RACK OF BONES WITHIN. He has also served as a hospice worker volunteer for Roseburg's Mercy Hospital.

James sold his old pickup truck that he had driven for seventeen years and now lives as a self-supporting Taoist bum. Smile comes from inside.

The Heart Has A Homely Face
by **Jim Victor Anderson**
Bookside Press | US Review of Books
Reviewed by **Mihir Shah**

From his intimate connection with nature to his unyielding practice of Tai Chi, Anderson's poetry allows a glimpse into how he sees the universe as it unravels in everyday life. Unsurprisingly, his upbringing in the coastal towns of North Bend and Coos Bay planted the seeds for a vision of life anchored in the movement of nature, away from the mayhem of the material world. In each poem, with such grace and simplicity, Anderson is able to capture the entrancing quality of nature and almost magically bend it to his will through an exceptional command of figurative language—chiefly similes, metaphors, and imagery.

A strong sense of interconnectedness with all of creation permeates throughout as Anderson opens up a time capsule for audiences to take a trip down memory lane. Early on, in "Echo," the emphasis on the word "Remember" winds back to the simplicity and blissful ignorance of childhood, the days of roaming free and truly being free. The Taoist perspective is apparent and adds a unique dimension to the works as it strives for an understanding of balance and harmony in an ever-moving world.

In many ways, Anderson's poetry is like that soft whisper carried by the wind, meant for ears inundated with turmoil and turbulence. Truly, every image is captured with such precision and knowing that the reader must surrender for this precious period of time and simply absorb the force of nature that is this compilation. Whether it is the description of silent meditation, "passing like the feet of children / running into distant darkness," or the migration of seasons in "The Homely Pint," as "winter running over windowsills," there is clearly a grace and ease with which the words come together that breathes life into each poem.

The heartbeat of the compilation is the poet's ability to use personification to create an instant and age-old connection between readers. Sometimes, it's the all-knowing mountains, while at other times, it's time apologizing to the wind. But in each case, Anderson allowing his audience to be fully present is undoubtedly what makes his work stand out. At its core, this is a liberating experience, one that urges readers to be at one with nature and to break free from the judgment and scrutiny levied by religionists.

Through poems like "Quiet Servant Earth," where rocky hills are personified to be listening to hermits emerging after years in the wilderness or hunting for the deeper meaning behind "Shanghai Bowl of Rice," Anderson's work is a cornucopia of color and inner reflection. Even the poems that seem mundane have a transcendental quality to them that ties back to Anderson's roots in Taoism. Interestingly, be it the wind, the moon, mountains, etc., nature is a primary character in Anderson's work, and on an overarching level, he succeeds in demonstrating nature's awe as well as fleeting time. In the end, all actions become one, and one returns to that from which they came. Overall, Anderson's poetry is electrifying. It is an ode to nature and one's search for inner calm and how, once found, life can present itself in beautiful ways, even while doing the most simple of things.

Printed in the USA
CPSIA information can be obtained
at www.ICGtesting.com
LVHW041208211223
766988LV00066B/2648